A BOOK OF LIFE

To Sherrye ♡
Every life is a book waiting
to be written

Katrine
Feb. 06

A Book of Life

Spiritual Journaling in the Twenty-First Century

Katrine Stewart

Quiet Waters Publications
Bolivar, Missouri
2001

For information contact:
        Quiet Waters Publications
        Bolivar MO 65613-0034.
        Email: QWP@usa.net.

For prices and order information visit:
        http://www.quietwaterspub.com

ISBN 0-9663966-8-5

Dedicated to all the delightful people I know who are trying to record their life's wonder-filled journey.

A special thank you to David, David, Alice, Elizabeth and Caroline.

TWO WORDS BEG to be typed on this page:

Just write.

CONTENTS

*"We are drawn toward journals
out of a craving for the authentic,
for the uncensored word and thought."*

~Mark Rudman~

BRINGING THE ART OF THE JOURNAL INTO THE 21ST CENTURY

There is no right or wrong way to keep a journal. Every life is different and therefore every journal will be different. It is my goal to guide the reader over and around the stumbling blocks so frequently encountered among frustrated journal writers in our time.

Listed below are a few voices of frustration I often hear:

- *The blank pages intimidate me.*
- *I can't write and I don't have any deep thoughts worth recording.*
- *I am afraid that my journal might fall into the wrong hands.*
- *Journal writing is boring and leads to self-absorption.*
- *There is no time for it.*

Many of these objections stem from an antiquated notion of what journals should really look like: a Victorian kind of notebook filled with page upon page of lengthy, hand-written personal observations. Quite truthfully, the popular nineteenth century diary often does resemble a spare-time luxury product of the leisure class. It tends to be boring and unappealing to contemporaries who have survived Y2K and long to streamline their lives (and their journals) to a slicker, less time-consuming, more honest version. Many of us want to face head on the real issues in life and not waste our creative energy on flowery descriptions of a seaside resort. After all, what are travel guides intended for?

The Tools of the Trade

Let us briefly look at the available materials before discussing problems and frustrations. The modern writer has many more options than previous generations to break out of the generic journal mold. This text does not distinguish between a journal and a diary. Both words describe life's daily journey, a written safari, so to speak. One is rooted in French, the other in Latin.

TRADITIONALLY, A JOURNAL is a book with blank pages, lined or unlined. Browse for a journal you like. The number of available journals in the bookstores is ever increasing. I believe this indicates a growing need to give personal meaning and cohesion to our fragmented modern lives. Perhaps one of the lovely journals on the shelf simply jumps out at you because of its color or format or the picture on its cover. Buy it! Spiral-bound, medium-sized notebooks with a sturdy cardboard backing work well. Choose one that you can easily put in your briefcase or bag wherever you go. The spirals and cardboard help you to flip it open and over for a hard writing surface whenever you need it.

Catch your mood in the color of your writing pens. Look for writing utensils that glide easily over the page. It's amazing how a scratchy pen can deter you from putting down some "flowing" thoughts, just like a dam can bottle up a river. On an angry day, you may find yourself scribbling furiously with the bold strokes of a red marker. Muddy, murky, depressing days tend to lead me to a dirty brown. Purple is my color of choice when something wonderful and out of the ordinary happens. Color adds another dimension to your power of personal expression, –even if you have a hard time finding the right words. Watch with fascination how the handwriting changes according to your color and mood.

"I'll be hanged if I am not in a humor for shedding ink tonight – feel as if I could scribble, scribble, scribble to the extent of a quart bottle full."

~George Templeton Strong~

Double stick tape and a pair of scissors will come in handy as you comb and edit the avalanche of paper materials that roll into and over your life. Glean what you can for your journal. This abundance of paper is a luxury of our time. Images speak louder than words. Use whatever comes your way, whether it is a magazine picture that speaks to your heart or a silly cartoon that makes you laugh. Stickers are yet another form of non-verbal expression that may be appealing.

Choose a personal theme for your journal that fits your present stage in life.

MANY YEARS AGO, I PURCHASED a journal with an inspiring painting of trees on its cover page. Almost by itself, it turned into a tree journal with many personal reflections (written in various shades of green and brown) on the meaning of trees in my life, interspersed by sketches, art prints, email and magazine clippings, bits of poems and songs, just to name a few. I thought of the people who had become symbolic trees for me and was fascinated by the fact that they all turned out to be male mentor figures. Soon, thereafter, I encouraged the participants in a seminar in Virginia to choose their own themes. What a joy it was to explore and research gardens, hands, seeds, birds, flowers, spring, desert, and oasis together, and cross-fertilize each other's journals! We made use of concordances and other resource books and had much fun with our exciting new discoveries, references, and symbolic meanings.

Since then, I have written journals on open doors–open windows, roses in my desert, vessels, dialogue, and the current one is on Trinidad. (At the time of my writing we just moved to this beautiful Caribbean island. Trinidad means Trinity, which lends a spiritual dimension to this journal. I am also looking at various things that come in threes in my life, such as my three daughters.) At retreats and workshops others have chosen puzzles, new beginnings, rocks, roots, wings, windows, gates, desert, letting go, empty canvas, bridges, things that start with the letter "S," water, light, dance, tapestry, sunsets as their themes— just to name a few.

"Does everything in my journal have to be about the theme?"

No, it is like the title of a book. The theme gives you a red line of cohesion that winds itself through your writings. It gives you a hook to hang your thoughts on. It helps you to integrate rather than dis-integrate.

"When am I finished with my theme?"

The theme will never be finished or exhausted. A good place for you to finish is when you have filled your journal. Often, by that time, you have a very good idea of what theme you would like to explore in your next journal.

"Should my journal only reflect the present?"

Don't get stuck in the present. Go back to childhood memories that are related to your journal theme. Shape your dreams for the future into words.

"I began these pages for myself, in order to think out my own particular pattern of living, my own individual balance of life, work, and human relationships. And since I think best with a pencil in my hand, I started naturally to write."

~*Anne Morrow Lindbergh*~

My journal is a room of my own where I am always welcome.

Every life is a book waiting to be written.

Many of us have become lazy in formulating our own thoughts. Why should we even try? Authors and TV personalities and movie actors and magazines are communicating for us. We let them put our thoughts into words. The more people we can quote (more or less accurately), the more interesting and well rounded we sound. In our day of instant information, it is indeed a luxury to think one very own thought to the end.

Explore what really happens when you read or hear a quote that deeply rings true to you. Actually, it means someone else has struggled to articulate that truth for you. Why not use your journal as fertile soil for formulating and nurturing your own personal insights? You deprive yourself and others if you are not willing to fight this battle for individual expression. Enjoy discovering your own voice and putting words to your own life's journey. Let your journal become a personal computer printout of all the data that feeds into your brain and heart day after day.

"If you cannot express yourself on any subject, struggle until you can. If you do not, someone will be the poorer all the days of his life."

~Oswald Chambers~

Do not think you have to write every day.

Keep your journal at hand and simply write when you feel like it. You may find yourself writing every day during a trip or when you are inwardly working through some difficult issues. Then again, you may not write for a month. In general, I try to find at least one time during the week when I can enter a snapshot of my current joys and concerns into my journal. You may want to keep a special basket or drawer or folder for items that come your way regarding your journal theme. Find a place in your home that invites you to write. Set a weekly date with yourself.

*"I sit in bed with a big breakfast and then I write.
I like that."*

~Katherine Hepburn~

The Blank Book Syndrome

Do the empty pages of a brand new journal practice a certain spell on you? Or might you even have an entire collection of those empty books simply waiting for your wonderful insights? Finally, one day, the right time has arrived. You sit down in a quiet place and write a few lines in your beautiful new book with the best handwriting you can muster. Then you proudly allow yourself to read over your first entry. Your heart sinks. Nothing extraordinary there. No deep insights. No Shakespearean wit. Just plain, old, boring you.

And many would-be journal writers never get beyond this frustrating, first-time page to face encounter with their own "unexciting" self. When you hit this block, try flow-writing. Let your hand put down what is on your mind, no matter how silly or garbled or incomplete. Fill a page or two before you even look back. Remind yourself that you are writing a personal journal and that no one is looking over your shoulder.

"To write honestly and with all our powers is the least we can do, and the most."

~Eudora Welty~

"I can't write."

OUR JOURNAL IS A BOOK written by you and for you. It need not be perfect. No one is grading you on spelling, vocabulary, style, or sentence structure. Follow the voice of your heart and don't try to please your English teacher from twenty years ago! In my seminars, I often witness a tremendous block to writing that sadly developed sometime during childhood.

Either a curious parent violated the sacred privacy of a journal or a teacher made some negative statement about inadequate writing skills. Invoke the negative voices that may have told you that you can't write. Write about them! Pin down the ghosts of the past by describing their upsetting behavior and their hurtful words. One lady told me that, as a little girl, she had surprised her mother reading her big sister's diary. The consequences for her sister were terrible. To this day, that lady always hit an invisible wall when she tried to write down anything about her own feelings. Tears streamed down her face when she was able to voice her memories and her pain from so long ago. The dam broke and her journal began.

"I don't have any deep thoughts worth recording."

Beware of the need to be perfect. "Perfectionism is a thief," someone has said. We are robbed of what might have been when we let the quiet voice of self-doubt and discouragement shut us down. Just write. Later on, you can "collect the diamonds from the dust heap" as Virginia Woolf phrased it so aptly in her own journal. We all long for significance and therefore want to write significant things. Think of your journal as a collecting place for the pieces in your life.

"Arrange whatever pieces may come your way..."
~Virginia Woolfe~

Put in the little pebbles, whether they are post-it phone messages, movie tickets, or an old photograph. In one or two sentences, try to explain why these items are significant to you. Personalize the "scraps" of your life. Behold, a wonderful thing will happen before your own eyes. The bits and pieces will turn into a mosaic of truth, easily transcending the limits of time and space and circumstances. Anne Frank created a world of her own in her diary that literally burst the horrible, narrow walls of her confinement and her all too short life.

"I am afraid that my journal might fall into the wrong hands."

Your journal is private. Absolute honesty requires absolute privacy. One question I often ask during seminars is this: "Who are you most afraid of to read your journal?" Overwhelmingly the answers name either a husband or wife or significant other. It is a stupendous fact. Those we are closest to and who know us best, we fear the most. I have spent much time pondering this phenomenon. It must have something to do with the fact that we are most vulnerable to those who know and understand us the best. Their scrutiny is the hardest to face.

POTENTIALLY CURIOUS READERS may be kept at bay by the words: "This is a very private journal. If you read beyond this page you are trespassing!" written on the first page of your journal. Put down an address or phone number in case you forget the journal somewhere. Some of you may still feel the need to hide or lock away the journal in a trunk, or a drawer, or a safe.

No need to feel guilty. You are on a search for a new kind of emotional honesty and truth as you begin to record your authentic voice. No wonder you are disconcerted about this exploratory journey to the unseen regions of your life's iceberg. Those you are close to are often terrified that your real voice might upset the perilous status quo in a relationship. A Titanic-sized disaster may loom between you. The lower, subconscious dimensions of your living and floating iceberg are something you have to put into words for yourself first, before you can even attempt to articulate them to your partner. The journal is a tool for lifting the unseen and non-tangible aspects of your life up to the surface, and clarifying them and defining them. This is very similar to the verbal therapeutic process that happens in a counselor's office, except that it is far less expensive, and one hundred times more real and accessible to you.

"If everyone journaled regularly and deeply   there would be less traffic to psychotherapists."

~Janet Taylor~

"Writing is work, communication, and therapy: all of them. Not therapy in the pop psychology sense, but in the sense of clarifying muddled thought, of seeing a photo appear in the developing bath, of transforming what is whispered in the ear, in the dark, into something ready for the housetops."

~Dr. Ray Downing~

"Journal writing leads to self-absorption."

MANY THINK THAT WRITING in a journal is somewhat akin to examining your own belly button, or like peeling the onion of your soul, layer for layer, down to a disappointingly empty core. It is important here to distinguish between unhealthy egotism, and a healthy search for meaning and significance beyond our own shadow. Oddly enough, egotism and a pathetic need for attention often set in when the personal quest for meaning and significance has turned sour.

All persons long for a positive sense of self, an identity to be proud of. When it cannot be found in good places, it is looked for in many not so good places. Often, job or family roles, or affairs make up the outside scaffolding that props up the precious and precarious edifice of the self. Woe to that edifice when retirement, or an empty nest, or the ending of a relationship strip it of its scaffolding! The journal is a safe place to explore who we are apart from the roles we play. It can help us to see life as a journey starting from where we are to who we truly are.

Legitimate fear sets in when our quest for meaning leads us to a disconcerting face-to-face encounter with the "self." It is this fear that I am trying to address. It is this fear that keeps many from writing even one word in a journal. We try to remain in our building's safe basement, so we won't even have to confront what might happen if the scaffolding of intelligence, youth, beauty, health, achievement, friends, and what not is removed from the upper regions of our life's structure. Men love to hide in their basements behind newspapers, sports, and questionable humor. Women find other creative excuses that fall somewhere under general busyness and an over-committed schedule. Most any activity becomes more important than taking time for oneself.

"Writing is a process in which we discover what lives in us.
The writing itself reveals to us what lives in us.
The deepest satisfaction of writing is precisely that it opens
up new spaces within us of which we were not aware
before we began to write."

~Henri Nouwen~

Only when you are willing to roam and explore the "interior castle," as Teresa of Avila calls it, with its beautiful turrets and its dark, ugly chambers—only then can you find the voice that is uniquely your own. The journal will help you in this process. Once you are able define what your life's edifice is like, its history and its purpose for the future will also come into focus. And when your building can stand on its own without the scaffolding of projected roles and masks, then you can truly reach out to others and not be afraid of pulling them down along with your own shaky, crumbling walls.

Early this morning, I walked up a nearby hillside on Lady Chancellor Road in our new hometown of Port of Spain, Trinidad. First, heavy brush, and the colorful trees and plants of the rain forest covered any kind of view. After I walked about twenty more minutes and rounded a curve, a magnificent view of the ocean and the port city below spread out before me. This sweeping sight entirely changed my perspective of where I had come from. I had busied myself with moving into our new house day after day and not even mentally grasped that we lived on an island with a vast ocean all around us. The "tyranny of the urgent" had reduced my vision to the blinder view of a horse. Had I not gone up a little ways beyond my comfort zone, I would not have seen and recognized the boundaries of the very island we live on.

THIS PICTURE WORKS ALSO for the "walk of the soul" we allow ourselves to take in our journals. It is an uphill march to grander vistas of the little world we actually live in. Was it self-absorption that led me up that hill? Or was it a search for meaning and for a new (and lovely!) vision beyond the context of everyday "valley" routine and circumstances? By attempting to describe a grander view of life in the journal, we automatically assume a mountain-top perspective, whether we like what we see or not.

"Whenever we write, we embark on a kind of heart-journey. Yet we are not sure of the destination. An act of trust is needed. We are often confronting the hidden part of ourselves. We have to be willing to meet the self that surfaces when we write."

~Emilie Griffin~

"There is no time."

Your journal need not become another have-to stress inducer that consumes time. Approach it from a different angle. As I said earlier, you need not write every day. Just invite the journal along with you wherever you go. Try writing a few sentences with your cup of coffee or as you wait in the doctor's office. See what happens. We always have time for the things and the people we like. Make friends with your journal. Rather than thinking of it as taking your time, let it be a confidante and companion to you. At any moment of the day or night, the journal is a patient listener that can help you clarify muddled thought.

In my turbulent and geographically ill-defined life, the journal has become a kind of personal ship's log, a place where I can find my bearings, sound the depths inside me, even when the high seas give no outside visual indication of where my life's vessel is headed. I have found that, on some of my busiest days the writing of a few personal sentences calms and centers me.

"In a way — nobody sees a flower — really — it is so small — we haven't time — and to see takes time, like to have a friend takes time."

~*Georgia O'Keeffe*~

Lastly, the journal is a timesaving tool for editing your life. Instead of putting every birthday card or letter you receive on top of some obscure pile, choose the one card that touches your heart and glue or tape it in your journal. Write below why it moved you, even if it's just a sentence or two. Discard the rest of the cards. Reread recent (or not so recent) letters and emails. Copy into your journal the one or two lines that really say something to you and state why it speaks to you. Tears and smiles are wonderful indicators for this kind of sorting and sifting. Throw away the remaining letters.

PERHAPS YOU THINK that you don't have enough time now to streamline your life with the help of a journal. Do you really believe others will have more time later to trudge through your paper jungle? On two occasions, I have helped friends sort through their mother's lifetime possessions while they were still in deep mourning. They were under severe time pressure and emotional duress. Do you think that is a good time to reread hundreds of old letters and documents and sort them out? Their hearts were torn asunder with frustration. No one can edit your life for you. You can't afford not to have time. Once you are gone, the baby gets thrown out with the bath water. The diamonds disappear with the dust heap.

Use the same editing process for all the countless other paper items that flow your way. Sort out a junk drawer. Clip quotes and pictures out of magazines that speak to you. Cut out the stirring movement from a concert program. Paste in part of the bank statement that says you've finally paid off your college loan. Try to include symbolic evidence of the inner and outer milestones of your life's journey. Always add your own insights. You will, in this way, provide truthful evidence of the treasures and the traumas you have encountered. You will clarify your own direction and purpose by discarding what is not important to you. And, at the same time, by making order in your life, you will enrich those whom you are closest to.

"Nothing feeds the center like creative work."

~Anne Morrow Lindbergh~

Allow me to share with you a journal entry that exemplifies this kind of continuous editing process over the years, over a life time, over generations:

Sunday in Juarez, Mexico, February 28, 1999

"Today I have been reading for the first time in my life Katrine's story the way my parents recorded it in their journals that they kept for me. Until now I had only browsed through the five small ring binders, stuffed full with ancient yellowing paper and small black and white photographs. Tears kept rolling down my cheeks as I read the handwriting of my father and my German grandparents, all now dead for many years. I put on the German Requiem by Brahms. It seemed fitting, Then I simply had to go and fetch my music and sing with the CD. More tears.

On my first birthday, already separated by continents, my father wrote me a letter that I now read for the first time as a 43-year-old woman. Here are a few sentences from the letter that struck me to the core:

Tschollire, Cameroun, August 1956

Dear Pimmelpammelchen! [Untranslatable...]

My wish for you is that something of the nature of this first year will always remain with you. Never again will you be so near to eternity, without the limitations of time and place, until the end when everything begins.

Your Father

Now, 43 years later, I sense that my father's wish has come true. All of my life I have had a keen sense of the reality of the unseen, the world beyond time and space. I am grateful that father took the time to put his birthday wish on paper."

OUR LIVES CONNECTED via an old journal page, despite the separation of death and of time. In my journal, I added a further tangible link to that mysterious chain of connection. Perhaps, one day, a child or grandchild will be touched and moved to add another link. Note that I did not translate and copy my father's entire letter. I simply extracted the sentences that meant the most to me and tried to briefly explain why.

The writer of a spiritual journal is driven by an intense desire to know God and find answers to the following questions:
Where did I come from?
Who am I?
Where am I going?

Motives for Keeping a Journal

Professor Thomas Mallon from Brown University has written a delightful and comprehensive volume on this subject called *A Book of One's Own, People and Their Diaries*. His insights into the history of journal-writing are as educational as they are entertaining. Let me briefly summarize the seven categories his research has led him to. Of course, few journals "cleanly" fit into just one single category. Use his list as an aid to examine your own motives for writing.

1. Chroniclers

These writers like to keep a journal of chronological events. They often sit down and write at the same time every day. Their entries tend to be more descriptive than introspective, and, for the modern reader, they quickly verge on the boring. Many Victorian journals fall into this category.

2. Travelers

Since earliest recorded history, this type of journal abounds. There is a great need to put down in writing what is new and remarkable and memorable on a trip. Even Caesar's *Gallic Wars* might fall into this category as the first copied and published "travel" journal. With the advent of printed travel literature and photography, the traveler's journal has changed in emphasis over the last hundred years or so.

Writers no longer need to describe what they are seeing. Instead, the focus of these journals has shifted to unique events such as civil wars or natural disasters, and to the inward journey that accompanies impressions and landmarks of the outward journey.

ON TWO OCCASIONS, I have greatly enjoyed experimenting with the usual travel journal format. While traveling by train from Bonn to Paris with my friend Lenora, we decided to keep a joint journal. We would independently record our experiences and thoughts in the same journal before reading what the other had written. What fun we had comparing notes on essentially the same adventures, yet as seen through two very different sets of eyes! In the summer of 1996 I drove with another dear friend, Donna, across the United States from Washington D.C. to our new assignment in Juarez, Mexico, across the border from El Paso. We used a similar set of rules for our joint journal. No looking at the previous entry unless we had first recorded our own impressions and musings. The theme for that particular journal became "roads and pathways." During our quiet time in the mornings, we would ponder the spiritual direction of our life's journey. We searched out postcards, songs, quotes, and verses in scripture that added new meaning to our pathway theme. That journal is a delightful record of our meandering, mid-life musings.

3. Pilgrims

A search for meaning leads the authors of these journals on an odyssey of the heart. I have devoted an entire chapter in this book to the spiritual journal. Pilgrim writers are not satisfied with the narrow boundaries of the here and now. They are keenly aware of an emptiness inside that longs to be filled. They explore their origins and try to articulate and define a purpose for life. Their inward search often leads on a journey straight towards God. Dreams and visions may also form an integral part of the pilgrim's journal.

4. Creators

The artists among us relate to this type of journal. It is a collecting place of word pictures and plot outlines for the writer, of tentative sketches for the painter, of unfinished musical themes for the composer. St. Exupéry tells us that "to live is to be slowly born." The creator's journal becomes a birthing place, a kind of receiving blanket, for the work of art that is yet in its conceptual, embryo stages. It is a safe and private place for experimenting with ideas and images, adopting them or discarding them at will. *The Notebooks of Leonardo da Vinci* serve as a splendid example. The inquisitive Renaissance artist tries to integrate his entire life's research into personal books. Theological discourse, botanical observations, bits of correspondence, sketches of the human muscle groups, astrological calculations and much, much more are permanently fixed by his pen in the over-sized journals. Had he given his journals thematic captions, he might have been more successful in categorizing the colorful array. There is evidence that he intended to sort them out for publication, but was frustrated by the monumental task.

5. Apologists

An urgent need to set the record straight drives the apologist to write a journal. Often, he has stood in the limelight of history and has felt deeply misunderstood regarding his public actions. Charles Lindbergh and Richard Nixon come to mind. I would not be surprised to see an apologist's memoir on the bookshelves in the near future written by President Clinton. Usually, journals are not written for publication. That would mean a contradiction in terms.

THE APOLOGIST'S DIARY forms a notable exception to this rule. I was intrigued to read that Georgia O'Keeffe told a friend that she regretted not having kept a better record of her life. "I wish I had kept a diary. I think I know now that my life is never going to look right." A perplexing dilemma. Who does she want her life to look right for? Hardly herself. It sounds like the journal she might have kept would have been an apologist's one...

6. Confessors

Why would grave robbers and thieves want to keep a record of their profitable loot? Why would a rapist want to write about his deed? Why would Victorians feel the urge to record their true feelings? Why would a US Senator keep a diary about his sexual adventures? The confessor's journal does not have to be synonymous with a criminal's journal. A deep need to unburden the soul shapes the driving force behind these journals, no matter what the reason. The private book provides a safe place, a quiet, trustworthy, listening confidante to whatever dubious deeds and/or feelings long to be spilled forth on the page. Should you find your journal heavily tilting into the confessor category, try to move beyond the paper to a trusted friend or even a counselor. You will be surprised to see how much groundwork you have already laid through your writing. Take the time to verbally follow up and deal with the dark and private issues at hand. Continue writing. It is a wonderful step on the path towards light and healing in your life.

I want to write, but more than that, I want to bring out all kinds of things that lie buried deep in my heart.

~Anne Frank~

7. Prisoners

It is not hard to understand why prisoners want to write. They long to occupy and express themselves. They need to set the record straight. They want to confess. They look for personal significance somewhere outside their four walls. There are many different kinds of prisons in this life. Some inmates are rightfully put behind bars, some wrongfully. Some, like Anne Frank, are hiding in a prison of persecution and fear. Invalids cannot move beyond the prison of their bed. Others find themselves entombed by prisons of emotional or physical abuse, or by the confining pronouncements of religious zealots. Anne Frank died in a concentration camp during the last days of World War II, but her journal lived. It will live forever. The prisoner journal is a wonderful gift to mankind, both for the writer as well as the reader. It transcends beyond the constraining boundaries of fear and pain, of uselessness and despair, of place and time.

THE SPIRITUAL JOURNAL

Our search for meaning and significance beyond ourselves leads to new and unexplored territory. In a spiritual journal, we set out on an inner pilgrimage beyond what is known and understood at the moment. We search beyond the limitations of space and time for that which is larger and more lasting than our own little, manmade world. We search for a clear vision of where we came from, who we are, and where we are going. Like many business companies, we try to define our own "personal mission statement." The hunger of the soul has replaced the hunger of the stomach. We long for an infusion of meaning in our lives. We long for a purpose, a reason to keep on living. The spiritual journal is a wonderfully safe place to embark on this kind of journey.

On August 3rd, 1998, in Divisadero, Mexico, I wrote in my journal:

> *"There are no words for the grandeur and majesty of the immense Copper Canyon that lies before me. God is here. Wave upon wave of rocky ledges and green valleys fall on their knees before His throne. I feel like I stand at the top of the world. I am a part of His incredible plan. I belong. A kind of inner death must happen when you cannot believe in a Creator-God who is larger than you. You effec-*

tively cut yourself off from the most powerful source imaginable of awe and beauty and joy and love and hope and forgiveness and healing. All you have left is your own dinky little intellect and personal perception of things. I am so grateful that I have come to know almighty God in an intimate and personal way through the living witness of Jesus Christ."

Why Keep a Spiritual Journal?

...to record God's story of my life

The German writer and poet Jochen Klepper tells us that his journal is God's story written in his blood. The word "write" is used 78 times in 69 verses of scripture. We are exhorted to write in order to remember the commandments, in order to learn a song, in order to be a witness. The act of "writing it down" over and over again is meant to help us learn and not forget. Teachers in the not-so-distant past believed in that very same method. (Incidentally, three books in the Bible itself, namely Chronicles, Nehemiah, and Acts, are based on journal-type entries.)

JOB'S WRENCHING CRY reaches us over the centuries: "Oh that my words were written! Oh that they were inscribed in a book! Oh that with an iron pen and lead they were graven in the rock forever! For I know that my Redeemer lives!" Every time I read these words, deep gratitude wells up inside me for the pen and paper that lie so readily at my fingertips.

"God wrote two books:
the book of scripture and the book of life."

~Augustine~

One danger of the post-Christian age is that it has allowed faith to become cerebral. In the great search for meaning, one must remember that God does not reveal Himself through our reasoning alone. He comes to us by the unpredictable path of our senses, our fellow human beings, our fragile health, our crazy circumstances.

"Comprehension of the invisible begins in the visible. Praying to God begins by looking at a tree. The deepest relationship of which we are capable has its origin in the everyday experience of taking a good look at what is in everybody's backyard. We are not launched into the life of prayer by making ourselves more heavenly, but by immersing ourselves in the earthy: not by formulating abstractions such as goodness, beauty, or even God, but by attending to trees and tree toads, mountains and mosquitoes."

~Eugene Peterson~

...to practice honesty and accountability

The journal is a place for the truth, for confession and forgiveness. It is a wonderful tool for drawing into the light what is dark and hidden. Once we have tried to define the submerged regions of the iceberg, fear evaporates. As many therapists know, we tame our monsters by naming them. Our spiritual journal is a perfect study or practice area for this kind of discipline. However, as true children of the light, we must go one step further.

Malcolm Muggeridge wisely states: "Every happening great and small is a parable whereby God speaks to us; and the art of life is to get the message." I like to think of it as putting God's email messages down in writing in my journal, but I have come to realize that no spiritual discipline is meant to be practiced alone.

"The unexamined life is not worth living."

~Thomas Merton~

We need to encourage each other, learn from each other, and be accountable to each other. This is why I so strongly encourage journaling partners and journaling groups. The spiritual search leads us on an unexplored path to incredible new horizons. It is a fascinating and disconcerting journey. Our illumined discoveries and new vision draw us inexorably towards community. We simply would burst if we could not share and witness what we have learned. The awe- and angel-struck shepherds in Bethlehem perfectly exemplify the phenomenon I am trying to describe here.

O N A MORE PERSONAL LEVEL, I have observed this same disconcerting "drawing into the light" process in my marriage. So many have come to me with great fear in their hearts that their spouses might violently react to the truths that they try to express in their journals. I know this fear firsthand. It is like a huge, fortified wall all around the heart that prevents the writer from putting down even just one word. Please do not be discouraged and do not give up. At first, simply write privately and for yourself in a safe place. This may not even be in your own home, and you may want to keep your journal with a trusted friend or relative. As you learn to articulate and define your own true feelings and the reasons for your fear, try to find a safe person to share them with. My educated guess is that your fear stems from the fact that you have even become dishonest with yourself. Especially Christians do not want to face and come to grips with feelings that they "should not be feeling," such as hatred or anger or jealousy or "inordinate affections" for someone other than their spouse. (Oswald Chambers so aptly chose that term to describe the delicate battles of the heart.)

"Pouring out one's insides may sound easy but it comes hard —especially when expressing personal feelings – in truth."

~Pearl Bailey~

The goal is simple: "There is no fear in love. But perfect love drives out fear, because fear has to do with punishment. The one who fears is not made perfect in love." (1. John 4:18) The dilemma is great, especially if the initial bond of love and trust has disintegrated. With the help of your journal, embark on the long journey back towards love. Begin to share the pain, the anguish, and the fear with other safe and non-judgmental persons. You may need the help of a professional counselor.

Name your monsters. Some of us are really good at sitting on a pity pot, with only our lamentable ego allowed as an audience. In a journaling group, you are apt to make the wonderful discovery that your monsters are not just your own. Others may be further along in the taming process than you are and can truly encourage you. Keep on prayerfully drawing your fears and your real feelings into the light. Go on a retreat. Open your heart for the warmth of God's unconditional love and healing.

I have personally walked this journey. To my great and immeasurable joy, my vessel has reached a new harbor of truth and love and safety in my marriage. Every now and then, I catch myself 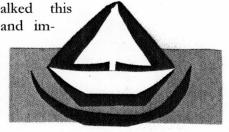 writing something in my journal that I know my husband might not agree with, or that I might have a hard time sharing with him. I use this as an immediate nudge to present the issue to him, to bring it into the light, to talk it out. He is not always right. Nor am I. But he is definitely better than I am at articulating his view of things. I use the journal as a tool for formulating my thoughts and feelings so that I can better communicate with him. And, in a wonderful way, the journal has become a barometer of the truth and the confident fear-less love that flows between us.

*"I needed to be shown the depth of reflection and personal
honesty that is necessary in keeping a spiritual journal.
Journaling allows you to get to know yourself and God
better, to dig below the surface even if it is painful."*

~Shelley Spencer~

...to explore God's mysteries as well as His specific purpose for me

Often, we only understand in hindsight why God has acted the way He did. Exploring God's mysteries in our journals turns into a wonderful quest for wisdom and understanding.

O N THIS SEARCH, you may also want to delve into the meaning of your dreams. In both the Old and the New Testaments, God often communicates through dreams. Why should this not be possible in our time? Commend your dreams into His care before you go to sleep, and listen just as innocently as the little boy Samuel did! If you are startled by the vividness and clarity of a dream, write about it. Share your dream with those you are close to or with your journaling group. Your friends may well be able to help you with insights on its interpretation.

"The longest journey is the journey inward."

~Dag Hammerskyoeld~

This is also a good place to explore the spiritual and/or symbolic meaning of the journal theme you have chosen. What are you learning? What direction is God leading you in? What are your waking dreams for the future? Remember that your journal is a good place to chart your course, state your goals, name the next harbor. God will not allow your life to succumb to the "haphazard quality" that is described in the following quote by Michael Crichton: "A day is like a whole life. You start out doing one thing, but end up doing something else, plan to run an errand, but never get there... And at the end of life, your whole existence has that same haphazard quality, too. Your whole life has the same shape as a single day." Could you imagine Mother Theresa choosing words like that?

Have you ever thought about how much your favorite authors have struggled in order to express what you admire so much in their writing? We have become exceedingly lazy when it comes to formulating our own search for meaning. In the glut of available literature, it is far easier to "buy" the answers that Chuck Swindoll or C.S. Lewis or Thomas Merton or you-name-it have found than come up with our own. God reveals Himself to each one of us individually. Just as no marriage is the same, so no God-relationship will ever be the same. We must fight to give shape and evidence to that unique bond.

"This is what I am, God's pencil. A tiny bit of pencil with which he writes what he likes."

~Mother Teresa~

...to integrate my faith and my life

God is at work within us. In our journals, we try to give words to His work. We try to get hold of the vapors inside us and make them solidify. And then, in some way, the solid stuff must be shared – whether it is treasure or trash. Sometimes only others can help to discern and make that distinction for sure! I like to say that, in my journal, the airplane of my faith lands on the runway of my life. I have had to truthfully describe some rather bumpy landings. Or the airplane simply flies over and does not want to land at all, especially on Monday mornings!

"Jahweh made my life complete when I placed all the pieces before him. When I got my act together, He gave me a fresh start."

~From Psalm 18, translated by Eugene Peterson~

Don't give up. The journal is a wonderful tool for creating order on the inside, even if it is a continual process. Life consists of making order. That is a lesson that especially young mothers learn. One practical tip I give to young mothers (or mothers of young children) is to keep little post-it pads all around the house. You can use this simple tool of our age to jot down thoughts whenever they occur, as well as those wonderful sayings that come straight out of the "mouths of babes." Collect the notes and put them in your journal at the end of the day. Actually, the same advice holds true for the busy pastor, the inundated executive, the absentminded professor, and most everyone else in between. You may also want to consider written phone messages as good journal fodder...

A Chinese saying tells us that the weakest ink is stronger than the best memory. Thoughts are like butterflies. They disappear if you don't catch them. Keep in mind the lightness and beauty of those butterfly thoughts. Don't kill them by pinning them down too tightly in your valiant attempt to express eternal truths. Remember, angels can fly because they take themselves lightly. I dare say, they can also smile at themselves.

Collect the fragments of your seemingly shredded life and watch a beautiful mosaic evolve in your journal. Gather courage to express what is unfinished, incomplete, and imperfect in your day. Allow yourself one sentence entries, whenever you feel like it, accompanied by non-verbal doodles and bits of coloring fun.

"God, in all that is most living and incarnate in Him, is not far away from us, altogether apart from the world we see, touch, hear, smell and taste about us. Rather He awaits us every instant in our action, in the work of the moment... He is at the tip of my pen, my brush, my needle — of my heart and of my thought."

~Teilhard de Chardin~

...to sort out His voice from the many others

In one of my recent journals I chose "dialogue" as a theme. On the front page I wrote:

"During a magical and bright moment of dialogue nothing else has to make much sense. The words spoken between two loving creatures bring life and enchantment of their own.

That is what this journal is for. I want to define and articulate those magical moments of dialogue that bring light and enchantment to my life.

But I won't shy away from other and darker conversations either. They are part of the whole. We are dialogical creatures, my brother Danny would say, and we are continually and at all times in dialogue with someone, —whether that someone is visible or invisible.

In my journals I find it easy to record my own voice. In this particular journal I want to try to listen better to the other voices in my life. Am I truly hearing what is being said or am I overly preoccupied with my response? My 15-year-old son Charles is convinced that I already have my answers ready before I even listen to him...

I also wish to try and hear my authentic dialogue with God and sort it out from the many other voices in my life. His messages are always true and simple and real."

Needless to say, this journal "mission statement" was one of the hardest ones to remain faithful to. And yet, I learned much in my attempt to distill life's dialogues down to their essence. As you pay closer attention to the voices you are hearing now, do not ignore the voices of the past. "What 'messages' did you receive from your parents?" is a question I like to work on at our seminars. In many instances, it can be difficult to untangle a father's voice from the divine voice, especially if you have had a wonderful pastor father who died young, like in my and my mother's case.

"Prayer is a heart to heart conversation with God
whom we know loves us."

~Teresa of Avila~

…to gratefully remember what God has done for me

Looking over old journals can be an extremely humbling and yet wonderful experience. Imagine the Israelites wandering in the desert, searching for the Promised Land, and being able to pull out journals and writing utensils from their camping gear? "They did not remember his power…" we are told over and over again in the 78th Psalm. I love to think that, if they had memory aids like journals, their frustrated meandering through the desert might have been cut short by half. We have no excuse whatsoever to forget the Lord's blessings like they did. In the age of computers and video film, our lives (and God's goodness) can be documented from the day of birth—and even before birth!

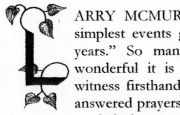ARRY MCMURTRY tells us that "…even the simplest events grow mossy with the passage of years." So many have confirmed to me how wonderful it is to look back in a journal and witness firsthand how God has directed lives and answered prayers. Our faith regarding an uncertain future cannot help but grow when we read about the reality of His faithfulness in the past.

*"Jahweh rewrote the text of my life
when I opened the book of my heart to his eyes."*

~From Psalm 18, translated by Eugene Peterson~

The Journal as Retreat

MANY OF LIFE'S CHALLENGES thrust us into front line battle. The journal can become a place of retreat for many a tired, daytime warrior.

When we find ourselves blindly hitting at whatever comes our way, bushes and enemies and burning issues alike, the journal provides a safe space for coming back to our senses. It is where the soldier can retreat to from frontline battle, a place where he more clearly sees the position and strength of the enemy and where he reevaluates his strategy. It is a place for gathering information and for setting new goals. It is a place for quiet inner renewal and for getting the commands straight by listening rather than speaking.

Above all, it is a safe place for resting, for healing, for nourishment. It is a refuge and a sanctuary. It is the special, private spot up on the mountainside where Christ went to be by Himself and pray.

TO LIVE IS TO BE SLOWLY BORN.
Antoine de St.-Exupery

"It is a private space of quiet and solitude."

~Lynn Klug~

A general fits his vital 'pieces' of information together into an overall action and battle plan. Artists fit their pieces of color and material together into a unique masterpiece. Life artists do the very same with their pieces of time and experience and vital relationships. Creativity is defined by how well we can fit the pieces together in a new way. Again, the journal can help in this lifelong process of trying to fit the pieces together, of trying to redefine battle strategies, of trying to get God's commands straight. Many fall into a trap of thinking that all the pieces of their life's puzzle are fixed, that they must always fight the same futile battles and the same cruel enemies. To the contrary, life is a wonderfully fluid, ever-changing stream that can flow into many unforeseen directions.

Little House   1/10   Amada

> *"Most people are conscious sometimes of strange and beautiful fancies swimming before their eyes: the pen is the wand to arrest, and the journal is the mirror to detain and fix them."*
>
> *~Robert Willmott~*

My journal is a room of my own where I am always welcome. The most essential things in life are invisible to the eyes. And yet, they determine who we truly are. Have you ever looked in the mirror and felt an utter disconnect between the inside and the outside of you? Try to describe what and whom you really see in the mirror if and when you are ready for a challenging journal retreat exercise. Go one step further, and try to define what God might see in that very same mirror image. You may have grasped in your head that He really loves what He sees. See if you can write that down. Sort His voice out from the many others you hear about your appearance and outward looks, —especially your own critical voice.

I was inspired to formulate the above exercise when I read what Anne Frank wrote in her journal:

> *"I saw my face in the mirror and it looks quite different. My eyes look so clear and deep, my cheeks are pink — which they haven't been for weeks — my mouth is much softer; I look as if I am happy, and yet there is something so sad in my expression and my smile slips away from my lips as soon as it has come. I'm not happy, because I might know that Peter's thoughts are not with me, and yet I still*

feel his wonderful eyes upon me and his cool soft cheek against mine."

ASTLY, THE JOURNAL IS a safe place to evaluate failures. It is no coincidence that, in the military, 'retreat' is often closely linked to a major setback or defeat. Richard Rohr claims that, after the age of thirty, we have very little to learn from personal success. It is in our failures that we are humbled, that we come to recognize the truth, that we develop character. Failure is an integral part of an honest journal.

Churchill defined success as "going from failure to failure without loss of enthusiasm!" Allow the reality of defeat and failure to enter into your journal retreat and watch its unexpected power to set you free. Who could better exemplify this amazing phenomenon than Christ! His life was one of utter failure in the eyes of this world, and yet, 2,000 years after He died a miserable death, the power of His words and His witness is still setting people free to live a new life. Failure and woundedness and defeat must be present in the journal that serves as a place of retreat and renewal.

Journal writing is reflective writing. By ruminating on the events and experiences, frustrations and joys of your days, you enable the original you to emerge. This unique you has been there all the time; reflective journal writing does not produce your uniqueness. But it can uncover this uniqueness, much as the process of tumbling and cutting and polishing reveals a stone's varied hues and unique patterns.

~Richard Foster~

Where to Begin?
Fun Starter Questions for Your Journal

There are NO right or wrong answers.

1. What kind of water am I? A babbling brook? A rushing waterfall? A clear lake? A muddy puddle?

2. What is my favorite color? Why? Has it always been the same?

3. Do I like my name? What does my first name mean? Do I like it? (Write down in different colors all the names you have ever been called, including maiden names and middle names and nicknames. Then color over the negative ones, outline and highlight the ones you like.)

4. Why did I choose my journal theme?

5. Which person in the Bible or in history can I identify with most at this time? What might this person be writing in his or her journal?

6. Where would I go on a dream trip? Who would I take with me?

7. What is a significant symbol in my life?

8. What is "home?"

9. What "messages" did I receive from my parents?

10. Can I find meaningful references for my journal theme in a concordance or in literature?

11. Why do I want to keep on living?

12. What can I write about my friends in context with my theme?

"You should work on projects that make your heart sing."

~Lady Bird Johnson~

13. What is my earliest memory of the theme I chose for my journal?

14. How would I describe my daily routine?

15. What are my greatest unfulfilled longings? Are there any dreams I need to let go of at this time?

16. What creative projects make my soul happy?

17. Is there a book or movie that truly touched me recently?

18. Do I remember the last time I cried? Why did I cry?

19. How have I seen God working in the details of my life recently?

20. What are the joys and stresses in my most important relationship(s)?

21. Where am I in my life right now?

22. Can I describe my spiritual biography?

Reflections on Writing

Following are a few encouraging quotes by more or less famous people on the "poor man's art" of putting pen to paper. Enjoy finding the statements that you can relate to. You may wish to copy one or several quotes in your journal and state why you do (or do not!) like them.

"Go into yourself. Search for the reason that bids you write,
Find out whether it is spreading its roots in the deepest place
of your heart."

~Rainer Maria Rilke~

*I Whatever is bothering you, write it down in a book.
Close the book, and a year later you'll open it up and say,
"Big Deal."*

~Joan Rivers~

*It is easier to absorb the large exterior events, and make
sense of them, than to grasp the inner disasters, which are
hidden from me (until too late, until implosion)
by my evanescent but thousand-times impenetrable armoring
of flesh and bone.*

~Lance Morrow~

I write to understand.

~Eli Wiesel~

*People who keep journals live life twice. Having written
something down gives you the opportunity to go back to it
over and over, to remember and relive the experience.*

~Jessamyn West~

I I *Writing is a form of therapy, sometimes I wonder how all those who do not write, compose or paint can manage to escape the madness, the melancholia, the panic fear which is inherent in a human situation.*

~Graham Greene~

It's often on days when I thought nothing happened that I'll start writing and go on for pages, a single sound or sight recalled from the afternoon suddenly loosing a chain of thoughts.

~Thomas Mallon~

Words and magic were in the beginning one and the same thing, and even today words contain much of their magical power.

~Sigmund Freud~

*VERYBODY IS ORIGINAL, if he tells the truth, if he speaks for himself... Consequently, if you speak or write from yourself you cannot help being original.*

~Brenda Ueland~

I write every morning as soon after the first light as possible. There is no one to disturb you and it is cool or cold and you ... warm as you write.

~Ernest Hemingway~

Every life contains within it a potential for clarification.

~Peter Hoeg~

*To me ... writing is addictive.
If I don't get to write three or four times a week, I start getting very angry with people, very annoyed.*

~Laurence Yep~

It is not easy to write in a journal what interests us at the time, because to write it is not what interests us.

~Henry David Thoreau~

For any writer who wants to keep a journal, remember to be alive to everything, not just to what you're feeling, but also to your pets, to flowers, to what you are reading.

~May Sarton~

Don't tear up the page and start over when you write a bad line...

~Garrison Keillor~

Life piles up so fast that I have no time to write out the equally fast rising mound of reflections, which I always mark down as they rise to be inserted here.

~Virginia Woolf~

Writing is an escape from a world that crowds me. I like being alone in a room. It's almost always a form of meditation — an investigation of my own life.

~Neil Simon~

I write to bring back what is gone, to relive what is lost, to make a mosaic of fragments.

~Minfong Ho~

"Be patient toward all that is unsolved in your heart..."

~Rainer Maria Rilke~

OPEN HEARTS,
OPEN JOURNALS

"The heart that gives — gathers."
~Hannah More~

Friends and seminar participants have contributed freely to these final pages. Browse through the various journal entries and enjoy the multi-faceted ways in which life can express itself. Do not judge by content, style or cohesion. Let the words speak from heart to heart, and in turn inspire you to simply sit down and write... If others can do it, you certainly can, too!

My husband just came home with a new scanner for our computer. The advertising logo on the box reads, "ADD THE POWER OF IMAGES TO EVERYTHING YOU DO." Allow this wonderful advice to add depth and dimension to your journal.

What color am I?

   "BLUE"

   Blue green, aqua, midnight

   Sky, ocean, and light

   Blue is my color. It's cool.

   It's serene. It's comfortable.

   Blues with red take me into purple, my rebellion.

   Blues with yellow take me to green, my refuge.

   But I always come back to blue, my balance!"

                                        ~Nancy Howell~

Why did I choose my theme?

I finished my "Passages" journal and am moving into one on which I placed "The Festival of Lights" image. The painting is by John August Swanson. It is a picture of many, many people carrying lighted candles. These people form a river of life — I mean light — that continues from the foreground to the top corners of the print where only streams of light are visible and the golds and yellows are picked up in the sprinkling of stars against a navy blue sky. It reminds me of both the Spiritual — 'This little light of mine, I'm gonna let it shine' and Hebrews 12:1 which talks about the cloud of witnesses etc.

~Mary Chiles~

"True holiness comes wrapped in the ordinary."

Anonymous nun

My journal theme is "Singer to the Songless". I remember leading songs for an Open Door Mission in St. Paul, Minnesota one hot summer evening. The setting was shabby and the crowd of hungry, disheveled men, many of whom were drunk, was not at all conducive to beautiful music. I sang but they did not sing along. They did not know the words. I served them food and then I sat to talk with several of them. They liked the songs and wanted to learn the words, so I taught them the words and they sang with me.

I see my teaching, my preaching, my serving, my caring, and all that I do, as singing songs to the songless. How can they sing if no one will sing with them and teach them to sing a new song unto the Lord?

~Larry Sydow~

I chose "Clouds" as my journal theme because recently I have spent lots of time fascinated with the diversity of cloud formations, and when I look at clouds I am able to remove myself from the hectic nature of daily life and be reminded clearly of the greatness of God and the beauty of creation. I love clouds because they fill me with lightness of being, with freedom, with heaven, with purity (as white as snow). New Mexico skies are so beautiful.

~Mary Trainor~

L ETTING GO. I chose this, as it is the season of letting go in my life. I must let go of my two sons as they grow. I have held on too tightly and my expectations are causing me pain. They must make their own choices and be willing to take their own consequences. Just as the trees must let go of their leaves at the height of their beauty so must I let go too and allow life to form them. I don't have a choice if I want to have peace. Letting go means not being in the middle of things and arranging the outcome, but allowing others to affect their own destinies.

~Bari Hill~

I finished my journal on "Time" and want to write a 'summary' or 'what I learned' post script. I don't think I'll feel a sense of completion until I do that. I started my new journal yesterday… "Let the Little Children Come to Me" (Mark 10:13). It will focus on releasing my inner child through play/creativity. I have started with vision and color.

~Nancy Howell~

I chose "Vessels" as a theme and put a picture of the 13th century silver Bertinus Chalice on my front page. I saw it at the Cloisters in New York and could not get it out of my mind. It is a powerful symbol for giving and receiving. I love its awe-inspiring age, its symmetry, its perfect shape. I love its sound base and yet its tremendous openness.

It is definitely a beautiful and precious vessel, one I can drink from, one that doesn't run empty, one that always stays polished, one that is as old as the world, one that is full of deep mystery, new life and wonderful healing powers. I do think that I have the legendary Holy Grail in mind, the cup that supposedly held the blood of Christ, gathered at His death on the cross. It is His blood that in a very real way is poured out for me from my precious dream chalice. There is true peace all around this vessel of mysterious beauty.

~Katrine Stewart~

Shared from a 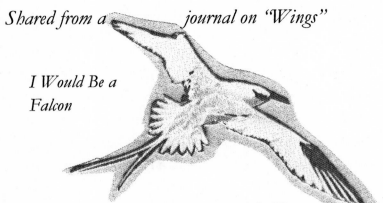 *journal on "Wings"*

I Would Be a
Falcon

I would be a falcon in the service of the King,
Sitting in quiet confidence on his right arm.
Waiting, ever ready for his time.
Waiting, for the veil to lift, for sight to clear,
Knowing his voice.
I would be the king's falcon, flung into the air,
Sure of his errand, having it in sight.
Swift I would soar with swept-back wings,
Knowing my purpose, to bring back the prey.

Prey in my grasp, I would return with free heart,
Back to my place, safe on his arm.
I am the King's falcon, walking on wind,
The prey my own will, surrendered and still.

~Susie Schneider~

From a "Garden" journal

After a garden tour. It amazes me as I feel the gardens. The discord of a poorly planned or cluttered garden brings a feeling of rush and a desire to leave. The sighs of stress die down in a peaceful garden bordered by a soft array of pinks and lavenders. God's natural air conditioning in a hosta garden on a hot & humid day. I anxiously await God's heavenly garden — no weeds, perfect weather — beautiful gardens calling for me.

~Judith Peterson~

About a snowdrop. The tiny periwinkle snowdrop is the first sign of the promise of spring. As the hard crusted snow still sits on the ground, this gift of hope emerges from the white snow and encourages us. The hard work it went through brings beauty and joy to the viewer. Help my hard work to bring hope and beauty to those around me Father. May I be as the tiny snowdrop.

~Judith Peterson~

"To cultivate a garden is to walk with God."

~Christian Bovee~

OLD PHOTOGRAPHS are a wonderful way to vividly bring back memories and seemingly forgotten voices into your journal. During one of our many moves, my father's proof for an official portrait fell out of an envelope. Below, you see how the picture became a part of my "Tree" journal.

Father said that sometimes young trees had to be tied to a pole so they would grow straight. This was how he tried to comfort me when I told him about the pain and loneliness I felt in boarding school.

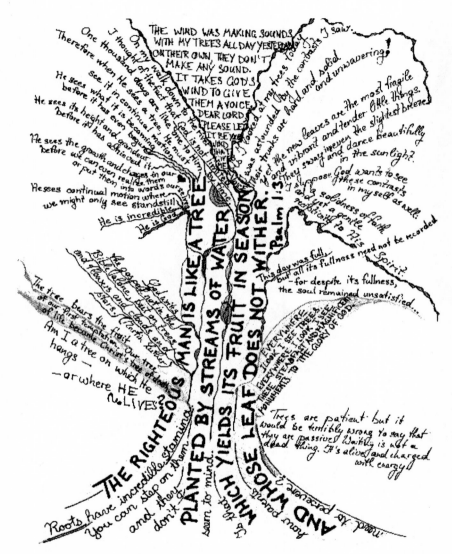

PLAY WITH WORDS. Enjoy the freedom of a blank page. Draw word pictures connected with your theme. Give your imagination loose reigns.

From a "Gate" journal...

My favorite gate: "Peter and the Wolf" had a gate that en-
tered the forest... and was a sign of adventure. This was also
a path that led to fearful encounters. It was safe behind the
confines of the gate where Peter's grandfather lived. Peter
took a risk and went through the gate. The Secret Garden
gate was so mysterious. It was covered heavily with a growth
of ivy which concealed a secret... a spot of beauty... a place
where magical things happened. This gate could not be seen
clearly in the wall. It was obscure and had a hidden entrance.

Both of these gates were some of my earliest memories of gates.

Where is my gate today? Where does it lead? Is it a gate with a latch or a lock? Does it swing in or out? Can I go back the way I came if I dare go through it? Changing directions is uncomfortable for me. I want to see that the pathway is familiar or at least well used. Gates can either be a hindrance or a way to something new and exciting.

I am looking for discernment and God's leading on which gates to go through... where is His will for me right now? Jesus says, He is the Door... the gate to freedom... the gate to green pastures. Today, I seek the entrance into a new kingdom for my life that is held in the strength of the Lord's guidance.

~Sonja Hinderlie~

"All truly wise thoughts
have been thought already
thousands of times;
but to make them really ours
we must think them over again honestly,
till they take firm root
in our personal experience."

~Johann Wolfgang von Goethe~

Travel brings new thoughts.

Had a beautiful day yesterday in God's stunning and majestic mountains of Glacier Park. I wonder if Elijah hid out from God in similar beauty, and if one can really hide from God when he is everywhere in Creation. Whether in the mountains, or the arid desert, or my backyard.

I can feel myself becoming dissatisfied with my life. I know any changes must be my decision and made from within me, or maybe I am hiding by doing nothing. I am sitting on Faye's deck and can smell the pine trees. Reminds me of walking out of the airport and being assaulted by this same scent. Maybe I will need to buy a pine scented candle to put on my table and be reminded of this precious time we four spent together for five days.

~Jeanne Uber~

OMEWHERE between Ozona and Fort Stockton, Texas, we've (the car and myself) reached a stretch in the middle of nowhere. Not even the radio scanner will pick up a station. What in the world am I doing here? The answer may well be that I'm binding my family together and maintaining cohesion in my own little universe. If that means that I still have to drive through West Texas many more times, I will!

~Katrine Stewart~

What kind of water am I?

Ocean waves are my kind of water — full of life and power, rushing up and crashing on the shore. Reshaping the beach and bringing fresh life ashore, constantly rearranging the patterns of whirlpools and shorelines, bringing new adventure to those who walk the shore.

~Bari Hill~

I am a river. I am flowing along with a swift current. But when sticks or logs interfere with my current, eddies form and I tumble and spiral downward. I like the security of my riverbanks, but when I look back over my life, I see that my boundaries have changed! My source is God, and He pours me out into the world of a lake or an ocean to mingle and influence other water.

~Donna Forester~

I pray to become like water for God. As water I can take the shape of my container. I can flow with God's grace and love. I can be still and listen to God's quiet voice. I can bend and twist, fall, rise up, and retreat. As water I can take the shape God chooses for me.

~Nancy Howell~

Am I a fountain or a drain?

"I am a constantly rolling stream.
I can't stand to be stagnant
but enjoy brief times of quietness in shady (Geborgenheit)
places where my spirit can revive.
Life runs in me and through me,
being constantly renewed by the Water of Life."

~Larry Sydow~

June 1998

I feel like a rushing stream. There is no holding me back, but I don't quite know where I am going. It does not really matter. Despite the rapid current, I feel safe in the love of my God and my family and friends.

October 1998

I feel like a fountain, not a big tall, fancy and lit up one, but one that quietly overflows into various tiers and is really quite unpredictable, but steadily flowing from an invisible source. The sound of the overflowing water makes my heart happy.

~Katrine Stewart~

*"I am a slowly flowing, clean water
in a high mountain creek
surrounded by lovely little tundra flowers."*

~Mary Trainor~

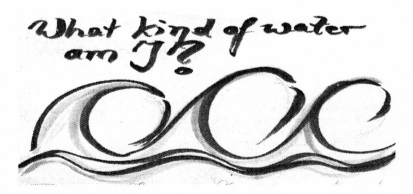

From a journal on "Rocks"

My earliest childhood memory of rocks: When I was two and three years old, I lived in Maine, and there was an outgrowth of rock in our front yard. There was an indentation in the top of it that caught rainwater, and I have a memory of sitting on that rock with my mother, floating paper boats in the little pool of water.

It is a warm, happy memory. When I was older, and we came back to Maine for vacations, I loved climbing on rocks along the coast. To this day, a picture of the rocky coast of Maine elicits feelings of peace and joy!

~Donna Forester~

Where am I in my life right now?

*Strange, I feel like I am not where I am. Continually
something inside me struggles with a lack of identity and a
lack of place. But that's not all-together bad. I feel like
I'm slowly and sometimes painfully being lifted up beyond
my conflicting needs to another sphere of unattached freedom and abandonment in the service of our God. Does
that make sense?*

~Katrine Stewart~

*"A humble knowledge of oneself
is a surer road to God
than a deep searching of the sciences."*

~Thomas a Kempis~

One Sunday morning I wrote:

*Sunday morning, very bright I write of things made clear
this night. Half awake and half asleep, my droopy eyes are
hard to keep. For closed or cracked they see before, behind
and back what only those of faith may see, when whispers,
mists or dreams break free. When God's clear voice seeps
in and on and through to lead the way that is not new, but
still is new to eyes asleep, unable or unmoved to keep the
Spirit's song, the Spirit's light.*

~Larry Sydow~

Another great journal idea

> *The bulk of my journaling in the past year has come in the form of special books I made for four special people (two children, mom, and mother in law) ...with poems, little incidents from the past that were worth remembering (thoughtful little things they did, fun things they did, creative traits of theirs). I put photos and drawings in them, as well. Each book was my view of them from a positive perspective: bringing to their face the wonder of their creation and their inner beauty.*

> *~Mary Trainor~*

Print out email

Dear Katrine,
What joy to hear of your plans! We'd be delighted to welcome you. We won't be doing much travelling this summer due to Austrian income taxes - so may the world come to us - and you mean the world to us.

Love, Daniel

My brother's e-mail message this past spring when I told him I could fly to Austria for my reunion in June. How I loved being there! My trip seems to have moved into a dreamy past when I look at my present surroundings!

Respond to art

Cup of Water and a Rose on a Silver Plate
Francisco de Zurbaran (1598-1664)

SIMPLICITY, SILENCE, POVERTY… is what comes to mind when I see this painting. The rose is so transient in its beauty but cannot be surpassed in its momentary present splendor. The water in the plain cup is pure and life giving. No artificial sweetener or additive is necessary. No mood-altering alcohol, no caffeine, no obscuring color. Just clear water. God can do the rest. And the plate? It is made of precious, long-lasting silver. It reflects the light that shines on to it. It holds the cup and reflects the beauty of the rose. It perfects the tranquil composition. All is well and in harmony with this picture and with my soul.

~Katrine Stewart

Put friendship into words

Monday afternoon

My foreign students think Lindsey and I are sisters. It would maybe take some time to explain to them that we're not sisters by the laws of this world – but in the Kingdom of Heaven we certainly are. I gave Lindsey a copy of this picture and wrote on the back:

Hanging in there together in Arlington

We're two Foreign Service wives being tossed between continents as if we were tennis balls... But it's fun to share our common experience and a deep friendship of the

The world is so empty
if one thinks only of mountains, rivers and cities;
But to know someone who thinks and feels with us,
and who, though distant, is close to us in spirit,
this makes the earth for us an inhabited garden.

~Johann Wolfgang von Goethe~

From an "Oasis" journal

Thanksgiving 1997 was an oasis of time. It was a time of quiet; a time of mending ... mending torn clothes and a wounded heart; mending a neglected house and a parched soul; mending neglected friendships and commitments. It was a space of time, an oasis of empty pockets, unscheduled and free to be molded to my fancy. Each moment was filled with healing moments.

~Nancy Howell~

From a "Sh-Sh-Sh" journal

(The following paragraphs are a wonderful example of how journal entries can lead straight into prayer.)

The picture is of a maternity ward. In the foreground is a mother looking with total adoration on her newborn child who is sleeping on her bed. It was taken in one of the former Communist countries, but I don't remember which. The baby is wearing a dingy looking shirt and an equally dingy blanket with holes in it. I titled it Love. —What is sweeter than a mother's love? The dear little one will know it all too soon if she doesn't already. A tattered blanket doesn't take away from her mother's love.

THANK YOU FOR MOTHERS who give and continue to give. Thank you for my mother who said she'd go on loving us even after she died. That never-ending love comes from You. What joy to know Your love as a mother. Bless all Your mothers this day with Your love.

~Sue Sydow~

A mother writes

Today is a red-letter day! My baby is 43 years old. How can these kids be so old, when I am so young! It is thundering and lightening this morning, even God is celebrating this red-letter day. Forty-three years ago it was Indian Summer. I can hardly wait to see my son and give him a hug and tell him I love him.

~Jeanne Uber~

Respond to the media

Oswald Chambers says, " My worth to God in public is what I am in private." <u>Integrity</u> is what we are when no one is looking. What kind of vessels are we? C. Swindoll

(Juarez paper Fri, Aug. 7)

Only the truth can set us free. May this whole scandal be a victory for the values of truth and integrity. Lord, make my own life transparent. Let your light shine through it and transform anything that is dark and dirty. You have the power to transform and you give me the power to transcend.

Da testimónio Lewinsky; podria alterar futuro del Presidente

"*Until we find our Center
we are at the mercy of every choice.*"

~Anonymous~

August 17,1998

Cover story: Car bombs ripped into U.S. embassies in Kenya and Tanzania, killing scores of people, including at least eight Americans, and wounding at least 1,700. David cried. They are a part of our tribe, he said. Many messages of concern were on our email. Truly blessed is the dawn that comes after the dark night of destruction and terror.

~Katrine Stewart~

A memory...

A special memory is of my grandmother who lives in a nursing home in southern California at the age of 101. She lives not wanting this life that she has but happy in that she is reliving her life through her memories — happy memories of the fuller part of her life. Change does not transcend those thoughts. She hears of my life in Owatonna and it becomes her life, sixty years ago. 'Do you still have so-and-so?' she asks. She does not want her past changed, so in respect, yes, it still stands the same as you remember, some of which is true. A calm smile, a soft head nod — these gestures tell me all is well with her as she drifts back to her silent memories of a happier life.

~Judith Peterson~

... and a discovery...

> *I have come to a great discovery and want to share it. My present journal, "A Journey", has been difficult. I leave it for long periods of time and then come back to it maybe to write gobs of words, or just a few. It is probably too broad a topic and my journal itself is too large. It is 7" by 9.5". My first was 5" by 7" and that was a bit too small. One I recently bought is 5.5" by 8.5" and I think that is perfect. This may seem a little thing, but it's little things that can drag me down. Perhaps this would not be a problem for another person, but it seems important to me. The new one is still a good size to put into my purse, it feels good in my hand, large enough to write more, but small enough to be able to stop at the end of the page. I like to fill the whole page with the same thought and sometimes I cannot.*

> ~Sue Sydow~

A conclusion

*No heavy concluding comments on this last page of my
"Tree" journal. Just much joy in writing and seeing and
loving and believing... The journal has been a faithful
companion and witness to our last busy months in Washington. Even at this very moment, David and I are at the
turning point of our trip. From now on we head west towards a more treeless landscape — the Chihuahua desert of
northern Mexico. But much new beauty only waits to be
discovered.*

~Katrine Stewart~

What is home?

> *Home is that peaceful place where God comes in and lets me know that all is well — that we are all connected through Him. I'm home when I surrender, in love, completely to the silence, the laughter, the tears, the friend, the foe, the joy, the sorrow, the mystery of this gift we call life.*
>
> *~Nancy Howell~*

The home is the only place of liberty, the only spot on earth where [one] can alter arrangements suddenly, make an experiment or indulge a whim. The home is not the one tame place in a world of adventure; it is the one wild place in a world of rules and set tasks.

G. K. Chesterton

T IS A PLACE OF LIGHT and hope and shelter for me. A place of happy secrets — not dark ones. A place of honesty and acceptance — even in hard times. I don't necessarily choose who is in my home but I do choose to love who is in my home. A home for me is not in one particular geographical place, but it is more defined by the people I am with and whom I feel safe with.

Katrine Stewart

"It is only with the heart that one can see rightly; what is essential is invisible to the eye."

~Antoine de St. Exupéry~

"Writing creates a sanctuary. It is a place where friends, although apart, can meet."

~Sylvana Rosetti~

A page from my "Dialogue" journal

All my life, the dialogue with my mother has been intense. Intense in its depths. Intense in its joy. Intense in its pain. We have worked very hard at making it an honest dialogue. Now we reap the fruit: joy, joy, joy!

"The core message of Jesus is that real joy and peace can never be reached while bypassing suffering and death, but only by going right through them"
~Henri Nouwen~

Just another way of saying what I had tried to express. Here is an excerpt of mother's last letter:

Some of the happiest hours this past year have been participating in your Journaling Retreats, Katrine. You have taught me that one of the purposes of a journal is to bring things into focus, making my faith practical in my daily walk. The theme of my current journal is "In His Time". I want to use it walking in step with Him. Not zigzagging. Not giving into the temptation of believing when I do one thing I should be doing another. To be where I'm at. Taking advantage of even small snatches of time to build memories for myself and others.

Ingrid Trobisch Youngdale

"Make two homes for thyself,
...one actual home
...and another spiritual home,
which thou are to carry with thee always."

~Catherine of Sienna~

The spiritual home, which Catherine of Sienna speaks of, is not defined by physical boundaries. It is an elusive place of rest, shelter, and safety right in the middle of life's storms. Many long to discover its secrets and intense, magnetic beauty. The journal is a marvelous place to explore the unknown territory of our soul's ultimate home.

BIBLIOGRAPHY

Broyles, Anne. Journaling. *A Spirit Journey*. Nashville: The Upper Room. 1988

Canham, Elizabeth. *Journaling with Jeremiah*. New York: Paulist Press. 1992

Chapman, Joyce. *Journaling for Joy*. North Hollywood: Newcastle Publishing Co. 1991

Foster, Richard and Jana Rea. *A Spiritual Formation Journal*. San Francisco: HarperCollins. 1996

Frank, Anne. *The Diary of a Young Girl*. New York: Doubleday. 1967

Hammerskjoeld, Dag. *Markings*. New York: Alfred-A-Knopf. 1964

Hocke, Gustav Rene. *Das Europaeische Tagebuch*. Wiesbaden: Limes Verlag. 1963

Macdonald, George. *Diary of an Old Soul*. Minneapolis, Minnesota: Augsburg Publishing House. 1975

Mallon, Thomas. *A Book of One's Own. People and Their Diaries*. Saint Paul, Minnesota: Hungry Mind Press. 1984

Moffat, Mary Jane and Charlotte Painter. *Revelations. Diaries of Women.* New York: Random House. 1974

Peace, Richard. *Spiritual Journaling. Recording Your Journey Toward God.* Colorado Springs: NavPress. 1995

Rupp, Joyce. *May I Have this Dance?* Ave Maria Press at Notre Dame.

Shaw, Luci. *Life Path. Personal and Spiritual Growth through Journal Writing.* Portland, Oregon: Multnomah. 1991

Von der Heyden-Rynsch, Verena. *Belauschtes Leben.* Duesseldorf;Zuerich: Artemis und Winkler, 1997

PICTURE INDEX

Ideas for the illuminated capital letters T, M, Y, P, O, L, E, were taken from a book by Patricia Carter called *Illuminated Letters*, published by Search Press in Great Britain in 1991. (Wellwood, North Farm Road, Turnbridge Wells, Kent TN2 3DR). I drew the letters myself and slightly altered the size and design and scanned them into the manuscript.

p. 27 Drawing no. 9. 1915. Charcoal by Georgia O'Keeffe. From a book edited by Doris Bry called *Some Memories of Drawings*, published by the University of New Mexico Press in Albuquerque in 1988.

p. 39 a picture of Anne Frank that I cut out of a magazine many years ago...

p. 40 card of a small writing angel statue, Coleccion foto-grafica "Tiempo de Angeles", Domenico Casasanta, Coleccion Biblioteca Nacional, Todos los Derechos Reservados, Impreso in Impresos Concentra, C. A., Venezuela 1995

p. 43 "Die Hände der Gepa aus dem Naumburger Dom." In: *Hände als Symbol und Gestalt* by Hanna and Ilse Jursch (ed.), (Stuttgart: Ehrenfried Klotz Verlag, 1967), p. 123. Photographed by Franz Stoedtner (Berlin).

p. 45 card of leaf, Georgia O'Keeffe, *Pattern of Leaves,* c. 1923, Oil on canvas, copyright 1996, The Philips Collection, Washington, D.C. (acc. no. 1447)

p. 56 picture of lady leaning on tree, from *May I Have this Dance?* by Joyce Rupp, published by Ave Maria Press at Notre Dame. The illustrator is Judith Veeder.

p. 59 picture of flying horse is by my friend Margaret Amado.

p. 65 card of rising (or setting) sun, Georgia O'Keeffe, *Red Hills, Lake George,* 1927, Oil on canvas, copyright 1995, The Philips Collection, Washington, D.C. (acc. no. 1450).

All the other "art" is by the author.

QUIET WATERS PUBLICATIONS

P.O. Box 34, Bolivar MO 65613-0034
http://www.quietwaterspub.com
Email: QWP@usa.net

Other titles from Quiet Waters Publications:

I Loved A Girl

By Walter Trobisch

'Last Friday, I loved a girl—or as you would put it, I committed adultery.' This deeply moving story of a young African couple is Walter Trobisch's first book. It has become a classic with its frank answers to frank questions about sex and love. Its tremendous worldwide success led Walter and Ingrid Trobisch to leave their missionary post in Cameroun and start an international ministry as marriage and family counselors.

ISBN 0-9663966-0-X

Miracle At Sea

By Eleanor Anderson

In 1941, more than 120 American missionaries had embarked on the ill-fated Egyptian liner Zamzam, including Mrs. Danielson with her six children who planned to join her missionary husband in Africa. The vessel was sunk by a German raider off the African coast. Eleanor Anderson, one of the surviving Danielson daughters, tells the story of the events leading up to the sinking and of the family's miraculous rescue.

ISBN 0-9663966-3-4

On Our Way Rejoicing

By Ingrid Trobisch

Ralph Hult had embarked on the ill-fated *Zamzam* as well. After returning to the US, he set out for Tanzania the following year, where he died unexpectedly. His daughter, Ingrid Trobisch, tells the story of what happens when God takes away the father of ten children. A whole family is called to service and sent into the world. The story surges with movement, partings and reunion, sorrows and joys, adventure and romance, shining courage, and above all, the warm love that knits together a large Christian family.

ISBN 0-9663966-2-6

Daktari Yohana

By John Hult

These captivating stories describe the true experiences of a missionary doctor in Tanzania, East Africa. Dr. John Hult is the brother of Ingrid Trobisch. If you love Africa, you will enjoy this book.

ISBN 0-9663966-5-0

The Adventures Of Pumpelhoober

By David Trobisch, illustrated by Eva Bruchmann

"In Austria they call someone who has a lot of bad luck, 'Pumpelhoober.' I, too, often have bad luck," Ingrid Trobisch's nine year old son David explains his nickname. This humorous children's book tells the story of the Trobisch family in Africa from the perspective of a child.

ISBN 0-9663966-4-2

Printed in the United States
43418LVS00003B/208-240

9 780966 396683